HOW NOT TO BACKSLIDE

IN 30 DAYS OR LESS

WORKBOOK STUDY GUIDE

**How Not to Backslide
In 30 Days or Less
WORKBOOK STUDY GUIDE**

by Blanche A. Drayton-Robinson

Printed in the United States of America

Published by Lee's Press and Publishing Company, LLC

Unless otherwise noted, Scriptures are taken from the King James Version of the Bible. Public domain.

Scriptures marked ESV are taken from the Holy Bible, English Standard Version. ESV' Text Edition: 2016, Copyright © 2001 by Crossway Bibles, a publishing ministry of Good News Publishers.

Headshot Photography Credit:
Imari Mitchell @lampproductionsphotography

www.LeesPress.net

Objectives:

This Study Guide has been complied for the purpose of providing concrete information to help reinforce stability for every individual who loves and wants to grow spiritually in the wisdom and knowledge of the Lord Christ Jesus. You'll also fine specific tactics used by the devil, in ways he tries to keep you bound in situations that prevents growth and development. You will be enlightened to ways to avoid the trickery he uses to bring about defeat.

This Study Book is designed to be used with the Text, How Not to Backslide In 30 Days or Less and like the book it is based specifically on the Word found in scripture, to expose the devil, used in his evil works to steal, kill and destroy. Things he does to avert or divert individuals from growing in Christ Jesus and trusting Him. Not being made aware of his tactics one can become his victim. Subsequently, the chances to becoming victorious are lessened and stifled. Then the opportunities in becoming a productive member in the Kingdom of God is not realized.

When one is not made aware of some tactics such as some of those mentioned used by the devil, it could probably cause a lost in interest, causing the finished work done on the Cross of Calvary, provided by Jesus Christ may become of non-affect.

Some Songs are listed at the beginning and end of each Chapter for encouragement. Hopefully it reinforces your faith, trust and understanding.

Table of Contents

Chapter One
Week One - Counting the Cost – Christ as Your Buffer

Fill in the blanks!
Luke 14:28

Song: "Alabaster Box" by Cece Winans

"For which of you, _____ to Build a _____,
sitteth down first and _____ the _____,
whether he have _____ to finish it."

Build

When building anything it is always wise to secure a lasting foundation, the necessary materials, instructional information needed rendering you the ability to complete the desired task. Spiritually speaking, it's the same principle. You must first have a made-up mind. You're ready to fight. There's an understandable expectation, there will be oppositions from the devil from time to time. But you will already know you have the Victory.

Taking time to equip yourself with the necessary proven tools, is a must needed prerequisite to withstand and stand against anything that threatens to divert or circumvent your journey, in reference to Jesus Christ. When you build you take necessary steps through prayer, seeking and invoking guidance from the Holy Spirit. Studying and committing the Word of God to your heart.

Developing a prayer life is your greatest defense. Spending time communing with God gives the Holy Spirit the opportunity to teach lead and guide you into all truths. This point may be redundant and maybe it is, but I feel it's worth repeating because of its gigantic significance.

Reflecting on Luke 4:28:

What are your thoughts on this Scripture?

_____

_____

_____

_____

_____

_____

_____

Focusing on the first 7 days:

Day 1: What should you realize?

_____

_____

_____

_____

_____

_____

_____

Day 2: What should be a concern?

_____

_____

_____

_____

_____

_____

_____

_____

Day 3: What do you study?

_____

_____

_____

_____

_____

Day 4: What will you learn?

_____

_____

_____

_____

Day 5: Who must you call on?

_____

_____

_____

_____

Day 6: To whom should you seek help from?

_____

_____

_____

_____

Day 7: Whom should you spend time with?

_____

_____

_____

_____

_____

_____

_____

_____

The Value of Salvation

1. Explain in your words, what is Salvation?

_____

_____

_____

_____

_____

_____

2. Something to remember when it comes to your salvation, you should do necessary _____. Daily _____ is what you should do. Attending, _____, _____, be _____.

3. A very important activity or behavior is _____! You must value the _____.

Honeymoon Period

4. Why does the Author, calls your conversion the Honeymoon period?

_____

_____

_____

_____

_____

_____

5. What does the 2 Timothy 2:15 say about studying the Word?

_____

_____

_____

_____

_____

_____

_____

_____

6. What is the purpose for knowing the Word?

_____

_____

_____

_____

_____

7. Do you know how much Jesus loves you? Take this moment to express it then revisit your response later.

_____

_____

_____

_____

_____

8. What are some things the devil does to you, once you accept Jesus Christ as Savior? List a few of them before.

a. _____

b. _____

c. _____

d. _____

9. What type of person is he compared to?

_____

_____

_____

_____

_____

10. Why does God permit the devil to try his children?

_____

_____

_____

_____

_____

11. There are _____ in the Word of God.

12. Why is it important for you to study the Word?

_____

_____

_____

_____

_____

13. Understanding your trials and tests will cause you to _____

_____

14. What is it, the devil wants desperately for you do?

_____

_____

_____

Know How Much Jesus Loves You

1. How can you be assured of God's love for you?

_____

_____

_____

_____

_____

2. When you feel overwhelmed what should you do?

_____

_____

_____

_____

_____

3. What is it, you shouldn't allow the devil to entrap you in?

_____

_____

_____

_____

_____

4. List things you must do:

1. _____

2. _____

3. _____

5. What is the Proving Stage?

_____

_____

_____

_____

6. What is happening when you are put under pressure?

_____

_____

_____

_____

Call on Jesus to Show the Way

1. Why is it important for you to call on Jesus?

_____

_____

_____

2. What scripture God's Word provides, letting you know He's always there?

_____

_____

_____

Seek God and the Holy Spirit

1. Why do you need to seek God?

_____

_____

_____

_____

2. What is the purpose of the Holy Spirit?

_____

_____

_____

_____

Trials and Tests

1. What is the purpose for trials and tests?

_____

_____

_____

_____

2. Your trials and tests are _____ with you in mind.

3. What is God more concerned about?

_____

_____

_____

_____

4. What does Matthew 7:11 means to you?

_____

_____

_____

_____

_____

_____

_____

_____

_____

_____

_____

_____

Song: Father of Lights by Jesus Culture

Write your summary of this Chapter!

_____

_____

_____

_____

_____

_____

_____

_____

_____

_____

_____

_____

_____

_____

_____

_____

Write questions you may have and want to discuss with others.

_____

_____

_____

_____

_____

_____

_____

_____

_____

_____

_____

Chapter Two
Week Two – Where Your Strength Lies

Song: Praise Is What I do by William Murphy

Fill in the blanks:

"Then he said to them, "Go your way. Eat the fat and drink sweet wine and send portions to anyone who has nothing ready, for this day is holy to our Lord. And do not be grieved, for the _____ of the _____ is your _____." Nehemiah 8:10 EVS

JOY

Most times when joy is spoken of, felt or expressed its usually associated with something physical that happened causing a reaction within which pleases the emotional part of the human spirit. But, really, in actually that's happiness in the moment. The JOY in reference to scripture connected to Jesus Christ is what He did for the believer, is not to be solely associated on the level of happiness.

The JOY experienced should be based foundationally on what the Word says about God and His Son Jesus Christ, in relationship to the work completed on the Cross of Calvary which gives continual stability in Him. Considering, the Work, done through Him for us, should be the everlasting Joy that navigates us. The Believer should be able to remain consent until victory is won. This joy is the state we should remain steady in, rather we're experiencing fierce opposition or not.

Living in the Kingdom of God as the scripture says, "For the kingdom of God is not meat and drink; but righteousness, and peace, and JOY in the Holy Ghost." Roman 14:17 Our Joy can remain the same in any situation good or bad. When based on the Word, not our happiness at the moment. This JOY provided by Jesus will remain continually, under any and all circumstances. Knowing God through the power of His Holy Spirit, Jesus the Christ will give optimum victory. "Oh, the Joy that floods my soul", words from a song, just thinking of this fact is joy.

One of my quotes, "If God was going to fail, He would have does so by now." You, me and every Believer can rejoice, for the "JOY of the Lord is our strength". God's Word gives us the fore knowledge knowing He has given us victory over any and all things.

JOY – **J**esus **O**ver **Y**ourself

Trust Jesus to bring you out, not what you yourself can do!

The Next 7 Days

Day – 8: In whom should your faith be focused on and why?

_____

_____

_____

_____

Day – 9: What does it mean to be in fellowship with others?

_____

_____

_____

_____

_____

_____

_____

_____

_____

Day - 10: How can you encourage yourself?

_____

_____

_____

_____

_____

_____

_____

Day – 11: What are reasons that can cause you to give up?

_____

_____

_____

_____

_____

_____

Day – 12: Why is it necessary for you to arm yourself?

_____

_____

_____

_____

_____

_____

Day – 13: In whom should you be aware of and why?

_____

_____

_____

_____

Day – 14: How does commitment helps in your growth?

_____

_____

_____

_____

_____

1. What is essential to the child of God and why?

_____

_____

_____

_____

_____

2. What scripture encourages prayer? Write it out.

_____

_____

_____

_____

_____

3. Why are unanswered prayers a blessing?

_____

_____

_____

_____

_____

4. List ways you can get to know God on a personal level?

_____

_____

_____

_____

_____

5. Who is the father of lies? Why is he?

_____

_____

_____

_____

_____

6. What is Power?

_____

_____

_____

_____

_____

7. What do you need to know about the devil?

_____

_____

_____

_____

8. What does it mean, walking by faith?

_____

_____

_____

_____

_____

9. Write out 2 Corinthians 10:4. Explain what it means.

_____

_____

_____

_____

_____

_____

10. What does the Bible teach about vengeance?

_____

_____

_____

_____

11. How can you win the battle?

_____

_____

_____

_____

12. What is one way the devil tries to make you feel like giving up?

_____

_____

_____

_____

_____

_____

13. Name something that can make you feel like pressing onward as a child of God?

_____

_____

_____

_____

_____

14. What lesson does your life teach may be from a Book some may never read?

_____

_____

_____

_____

_____

15. Write one scripture that proves God does forgive sin.

_____

_____

_____

_____

_____

16. Write what is the hardest thing that's difficult for you to forgive.

_____

_____

_____

_____

_____

17. Write the scripture that confirms the power of our testimony.

_____

_____

_____

_____

_____

18. Name some ways that brings about our testimonies.

_____

_____

19. What is the reason for expecting the unexpected?

_____

_____

20. What does it mean to be redeemed?

_____

_____

_____

_____

_____

A Song for encouragement: William Murphy – Your Love

**** Write your testimony****

Chapter 3
Week 3: Developing Your Spiritual Weapons: "Don't Give Up"

Fill in the blanks:

2 Corinthians. 2: 3-5

"For though we walk in the _____, we do not _____ after the
_____:

(For the _____ of our _____ are not _____, but
mighty through God to the pulling down of strong holds;)

Casting down _____, and every high thing that _____
itself against the _____ of God, and bringing into captivity
every _____ to the _____ of Christ;"

We, the children of God will always be confronted with resistance. This is the warfare
we experience. Warfare is the activity that goes on when the Flesh (self) struggles
against the Spirit, wanting to disobey what the Holy Spirit will have you do in accordance
to the Word of God. The carnal things are fleshly. Subsequently, our weapon must be
the Word of God and not physical.

When the Word of God is committed to our heart is gives the Holy Spirit freedom to
operate and fight on our behalf. We won't have to conjure up and imagine ways to
overcome using our own intuition. Walking in the flesh is the human part of us walking
to please our own heart's desires. But submission and surrender to the Holy Spirit, He
rules and directs the path to the obedience of Christ.

Song: No Weapon Formed Against Me by Fred Hammond

The Next 7 Days

Day – 15: What is it you must understand about yourself?

_____

_____

_____

_____

Day – 16: You should _____ a _____
desire for the _____ of _____.

Day – 17: Who do trust to bring you out of your troubles?

_____

_____

_____

_____

Day – 18: You should _____ the devil is a _____.

Day – 19: Why would you say you need God?

_____

_____

_____

_____

Day – 20: What is the reason for Fasting?

_____

_____

_____

_____

_____

_____

Day – 21: List are some spiritual exercises discussed in this Book.

_____

_____

_____

_____

The Operative Word

1.) Tell what happens within you when development takes place?

_____

_____

_____

_____

2.) What does it mean to put on the whole armor of God?

_____

_____

_____

_____

3.) What does Ephesians 6:11 tells you to do?

_____

_____

_____

_____

4.) Why should you desire the Word?

_____

_____

_____

_____

5.) What does Ephesians 6:11 tells you to do?

_____

_____

_____

_____

6.) What does God allow the devil to do?

_____

_____

7.) Why does God allow the devil to attack you?

_____

_____

_____

_____

8.) What should you do when going through difficult situations?

_____

_____

_____

_____

9.) What is your greatest weapon?

_____

_____

_____

_____

10.) Why is your Mouth your greatest weapon?

_____

_____

_____

_____

11.) What is the devil's mission?

_____

_____

_____

_____

12.) List a few things the devil has tried to discourage you.

_____

_____

_____

_____

13.) Why would the devil want to discourage you?

_____

_____

_____

14.) Name one thing you can do for the kingdom of God.

_____

_____

_____

_____

15.) What does Proverbs 9:10 teach about Fear?

_____

_____

_____

_____

16.) What does the scripture teach about the narrow and wide gates?

_____

_____

_____

_____

17.) Write at least one scripture you know, God forgives sin.

_____

_____

_____

_____

18.) Write your testimony of a time you know you had to trust God.

_____

_____

_____

_____

_____

_____

19.) What does it mean to set you affection on things above?

_____

_____

_____

_____

_____

HOW NOT TO BACKSLIDE IN 30 DAYS OR LESS – WORKBOOK STUDY GUIDE

20.) Share your views on fasting compared to scripture.

_____

_____

_____

_____

21.) What does this Book say about boot camp?

_____

_____

_____

_____

Song: Jason Nelson – Love You Forever

Chapter 4

Week 4: Staying Connected; Relationship, Fellowship and Worship

Song: I'll Love You Forever by Tye Tribbett

Fill in the blanks:

Matt. 18:20

For where _____ or _____ are gathered together in my name, there am I in the midst of them.

Heb. 10:25

Not _____ the assembling of ourselves together, as the manner of some is, but _____ one another: and so much the more, as ye see the day _____.

It is necessary to come together because as the saying goes, "There's strength in numbers".

I believe, this statement in all sincerity, sums up the whole message about not forsaking the assembling of yourself because of the encouragement and strength that will be gained from personal relationships. If the devil can isolate, he can annihilate (rip off, slay, and demolish). You will lose the desire. Consequently, ceasing to please and seek after the things or power of God.

Seven More Days

Day 22: How do you build a relationship with God?

_____

_____

_____

_____

Day 23: With whom should you build fellowship with?

_____

_____

_____

_____

Day 24: What type of attitude should you have?

_____

_____

_____

_____

Day 25: How do you become a vessel for God?

_____

_____

_____

_____

Day 26: What is one fact you can state about the devil?

_____

_____

_____

_____

Day 27: What is at least one thing you must establish?

_____

_____

_____

Day 28: When you continue your relationship with God _____ _____
_____ _____ _____ for you.

Relationship

1. List some things that starts a relationship.

_____

_____

_____

_____

2.) Share feelings of your first encounter when you experienced God's presence.

_____

_____

_____

_____

3.) Why is it necessary to develop a relationship?

_____

_____

_____

_____

4.) Write what Jesus spoke in John 14:6.

_____

_____

_____

5.) Getting to know _____ the _____ of _____ is the
_____ _____ of _____ you or
anyone can _____ in your
_____ .

6.) The _____ relationship you _____
will be the _____ to your _____ .

Fellowship

1.) Why is it important to be with other Christians?

_____

_____

_____

_____

2.) How does it help you when you commit to God?

_____

_____

_____

_____

3.) In your own words explain 2 Corinthians 5:14.

_____

_____

_____

_____

4.) Tell how you can strengthen yourself.

_____

_____

_____

_____

"And if _____ prevail against him, _____ shall _____ him; and a _____ _____ is not easily _____. Ecc. 4:4:12

Worship

1.) What is worship?

_____

_____

_____

2.) List a few ways God can be worshipped.

_____

_____

_____

_____

3.) Give at least one reason why you should stay connected.

_____

_____

_____

_____

4.) Write in your own words what you think Jeremiah 18 is talking about and discuss with others.

_____

_____

_____

_____

5.) What is the greatest tool you can have to help you live victoriously in Christ?

_____

_____

_____

_____

A Sense of Purpose

1.) List what a sense of purpose details.

_____

_____

_____

_____

2.) What's the devil's reasons for wanting to detain or divert your attention?

_____

3.) List some ways the devil will try to prevent you studying.

_____

_____

_____

_____

Write your summary of this Chapter.

_____

_____

_____

_____

_____

_____

_____

_____

_____

_____

_____

_____

_____

_____

_____

_____

_____

_____

_____

_____

_____

Song: He's Bigger by Jekalyn Carr

Chapter 5
The Test

Song: All Things Are Working For My Good by Travis Greene

Fill in the missing words. Be sure to think upon its meaning as it pretends to you.

1 Peter 4:12

Beloved, _____ it not _____ concerning the _____ trial which is to _____ you, as though some _____ thing happened unto you.

1 Peter 4:13

But _____, in as much as ye are _____ of _____ suffering; that, when his glory shall be reveal, ye may be glad also with exceeding joy.

1 Peter 4:14

If ye be _____ for the name of _____, happy are ye; for the spirit of glory and God _____ upon you: on their part he is evil spoken of, but on _____ part he is glorified.

Strange:

Being prepared, you have everything you need to combat anything the devil through anyone tries to use to deter or confuse you. So, when things happen don't let it discombobulate you, use your word. The Word of God will show you and empowering you to remain victorious.

The Last 2 Days

Day 29: What are you going to check?

_____ the

_____ and your spiritual _____.

Day 30: What can you do to encourage yourself?

REJOICE! You have learned not to _____ in _____ or

_____.

It is my prayer that at this point, after reading the previous chapters, you are convinced that Hell is real, backsliding is serious.

1. What matters most to the devil?

_____
_____
_____
_____

2. What causes the devil to attack you?

_____
_____
_____
_____

3. Why doesn't it matter to the devil if you go to church?

_____
_____
_____
_____

4. What does the devil put in your path?

_____
_____
_____

5. What are stumbling blocks?

_____
_____
_____

6. What is the devil trying to do by putting stumbling blocks in your way?

_____

_____

_____

_____

7. A lot of things are said from the _____, but it's in the _____ where God looks and sees.

8. Write the scripture which shows God looks at the heart.

_____

_____

_____

_____

9. Complete Matt. 15:8

This people _____ nigh unto me with their _____, and _____ me with their _____; but their _____ is far from me.

10. Explain what Isaiah 29:13 says.

_____

_____

_____

_____

11. How does Jeremiah 17:9 describes the heart?

_____

_____

_____

_____

12. Tell how the Word and the Holy Spirit help us.

_____

_____

_____

_____

13. What is the hope of the believer?

_____

_____

14. What is the warning the Apostle Peter warns us about?

_____

_____

_____

_____

15. _____ are creatively designed by God to
_____ _____ and _____ you. But
the _____ tries to _____ them against you, to
_____ _____.

16. Fill I the blanks with words the devil uses to impede your growth.
_____, _____, and a lack of
_____ _____ with the Lord.

17. Write 1 John 2:1 as a reminder to encourage yourself when feeling defeated.

18. _____

_____

_____

_____

19. Tell what 1 Peter 3:15 encourages.

_____

_____

_____

_____

20. What are Red Flags?

_____

_____

_____

_____

21. What does PPT stands for?

_____

_____

_____

_____

_____

22.   Why is PPT important?

_____

_____

_____

_____

Song: I Believe by Jonathan Nelson

Answers to Questions

Chapter 1

Day 1: You should realize and appreciate the value of what Christ did, giving His life on the Cross.

Day 2: You should be concerned that you don't forget that trials and tests are going to come and many times after you've rejoiced over something profound or not.

Day 3: You study the Word to regularly to remain strengthened for it is your weapon.

Day 4: You will learn how much Jesus loves you.

Day 5: You must call on Jesus or the Holy Spirit for assistance.

Day 6: You should seek help from the Holy Spirit. It is through the Lord Jesus Christ, He teaches us through His Spirit.

Day 7: It is important to spend time with God in prayer and in meditation. His Spirit will enlighten and give guidance.

THE VALUE OF SALVATION

1. Some _____.

A. <u>Bible Study</u>
B. <u>Church Services</u>
C. <u>Accountability</u>

2. A very important activity is <u>Prayer.</u>

3. You must value <u>the word of God</u>.

Honeymoon pg. 21

1. It is the Joy you experience that is like no other. Things are happening just as you want to.

2. See 2 Timothy 2:15

3. Knowing the Word equips you to defeat the devil when he attacks. See Matthew Chapter 4.

4. Express now and revisit it your response later.

5. List things the devil does. <u>Aggravates</u>, <u>harass</u>, <u>stalks,</u> <u>agitates.</u>

6. A jealous lover

7. God allows the devil to try us to afford us the opportunity to know Him on a personal level.

8. <u>Treasures</u>

9. It is your ammunition in which you are able to fight with in order to defeat the devil. See Deuteronomy 8:1-10.

10. <u>Trust</u> <u>Him</u>

11. He wants you to walk away from the things of God, your personal relationship.

Know How Much Jesus Loves You pg. 25

1. The scriptures ensures us of God's love and our fellowship with Him.

2. You always seek help from someone like your Pastor or Spiritual leaders associated within those within your place of fellowship.

3. Do not let the devil trap you into negativity or devaluing what the Word says.

List things you must do:
1. Study the word
2. Pray
3. Find Support

4. When trials and tests come. How you handle them. Character building takes place during the process.

5. When you are put under pressure, it's a cleansing and polishing process, so to speak. You're being strengthened in your faith, in God to be a witness to bring souls into the Kingdom of God.

Call on Jesus to show the way

1. It is important for you to call on Jesus because He's your present help in trouble. Ps. 46:1 You are no match for the devil. He's too cunning. That's why God provided you help through Jesus Christ and the Holy Spirit.

2. We know God will be there because of His Word. Heb. 13:5

Seek God and the Holy Spirit

1. You need to seek God for Him to fill you with His Holy Spirit.

2. The purpose of the Holy spirit is to be your Helper. He will provide you the assistance you need to guide you or bring about deliverance when needed. He is the bridge between you and God.

Trials and Tests

1. Trials and tests serve many purposes and reasons, He connects us to God and His purpose for your life. They build up trust also getting to know God through His Holy Spirt.

2. Your trials and test are _____ with you in mind.

3. God is concerned about your soul and that you are saved. Your soul has attachment to the world. Therefore, He uses trials and tests to strip your soul from those attachments. Bringing your focus on Him and the plans and purpose He has for you.

Chapter 2

Week Two – Where Your Strength Lies

The Next 7 Days

Day 8: Your faith should be focused on Jesus Christ not what man is doing but rather he is doing and saying what the Word says. It is through the word your Faith will be increased.

Day 9: Being in fellowship with others, simply, you, taking time to get with those of like minds in order to be encouraged and to encourage.

Day 10: You can encourage yourself when you surround yourself with positive people, listen to encouraging music. Read literature that will enhance your knowledge and faith in Christ Jesus.

Day 11: There are always reasons that will cause you to give up such as, friends who don't believe as you do. Lack of study time in the Word and in prayer.

Day 12: It is also necessary to arm yourself because arming yourself with the Word and pray it is the way you will be victorious because you are in a spiritual battle. 2 Corinthians 10:3-7

Day 13: The child of God should be ever ready or equipped spiritually due to unbelieving friends and people who don't believe, they will try to disarm you of your faith in Jesus Christ.

Day 14: When you are committed you are convinced in death, burial and resurrection of Jesus Christ giving you the determination needed to remain steadfast and faithful to the Cross of Christ.

Prayer

1. List one thing that's essential to the child of God. _____
2. Write out Luke 18:1.

_____

_____

3. Unanswered prayers can be a blessing because God knows the future and He protects us due to prayers we pray uninformed. Even though its don with good intentions to find out later that's not good for you or you have a change of heart. The reasons vary. Just know, God knows BEST.

4. The ways you can know God on a personal level: through studying the Word, prayer, fellowship with like-minded people, Fasting, listening to inspirational music and other inspirational writings by Christians.

5. The devil, he is the father of lies. He uses lies to manipulate and confuse to issues.

6. Knowledge is power, it gives you the authority to control and defeat the devil in any and all situations.

7. You need to know that the devil is a liar! He always wants to deceive you by any and all means.

8. Walking by faith is trusting and using the Word of God to make decisions and sharing when your circumstances may look hopeless, or you can see no way out or know how things will turn out.

9. See the Bible to complete 2 Corinthians 10:4

10. The word teaches us in Romans 12:19 Vengeance is the Lord's. It is God's authority to decide the response to anyone of our deeds. For He alone knows the prefect results for every situation. Of course, the world has a different view.

11. You can win your battles by applying the Word of God, praying and talking with others of the same faith.

12. The devil will probably make you feel like giving up when you make mistakes or other things seems to be more productive. Read Psalm 73: 1-3

13. The one thing that will keep a child of God pressing forward is no different from anything else, which is prayer also communication with others of like faith.

14. Your life may be the only Bible others read that teaches them about Christ.

15. One scripture that shows God forgives our sin is 1 John 1:9.

16. Tell what's difficult for you. For me, it was forgiving myself.

17. Revelation 12:11, describes how we overcome.

18. Some ways you acquire testimonies vary; it could be through trials, tests or various situations God allows us to go through.

19. The reason for expecting the unexpected just keeps you prepared in that you are not blindsided. Your first response will be to seek God, which will not cause you to end up in an unwanted situation. If by chance you do, you will know you are not defeated.

20. What is means to be redeem, knowing Christ paid the ultimate price when He died on Calvary. We are no longer slaves to sin. We can have fellowship with God through Jesus Christ.

Chapter 3

Week – 3 Developing Your Spiritual Weapons – "Don't Give Up"

Seven More Days

Day: 15 You should always remember you're a sinner saved by God's grace.

Day: 16 You should <u>develop</u> a <u>sincere</u> <u>desire</u> for the <u>Word</u> of <u>God</u>.

Day: 17 You should always trust God and know that He will bring you out of your troubles.

Day: 18 <u>Recognize</u> the devil is a liar.

Day: 19 You are no match for the devil. He's too cunning. He has ways to trap us that we know not of.

Day: 20 Fasting I've found; it gives spiritual clarity. It helps discipline the body to be obedient to God. Also, you are clearer in mind to be led by the Spirit.

Day: 21 Some spiritual exercises to me are, Studying the word, Singing spiritual songs, spending time seeking God.

Operative Word

1. When you develop, your knowledge increases, your trials and tests are easier to deal with and understand. You become more aware of God's provision and protection to promote spiritual growth.

2. You've committed to the Word of God and you Use the Word to combat the attacks of the devil.

3. I feel, Desiring the Word of God is an assurance of a continual desire to seeking after God.

4. Some reasons, you should desire the Word is to keep you seeking, thirsty and hungry for the Word and studying it, to be in God's presence.

5. Write out Eph. 6:11.

6. God allows the devil to tempt us. Therefore, when we are tempted, we should know it comes from the devil.

7. We get know God through our difficult situations, when we are tempted, our trust is increased.

8. When doing through difficulty you should spend time in the presence of God. Rehearse the Word and sing or listen to songs that encourages your faith.

9. Your greatest weapon is the Word of God coming from your mouth.

10. Faith comes by hearing, hearing by the word of God. By speaking it, you hear it.

11. The devil's mission is to steal, kill and destroy.

12. List somethings the devil uses to discourage you. This is one I heard often, "It doesn't take all that."

13. The devil discourages you because he knows the great things God has instore for you and you will not win other souls for Christ. He loses!

14. One thing you can do as a child of God is win souls for the Kingdom of God.

15. Proverbs 9: 10 teaches, Fear is the beginning of Knowledge.

16. The narrow gate leads to Jesus, eternal life, but the wide gate leads to the world or death.

17. Write one scripture that assures, God forgives.

18. Write a testimony of a time you had to trust God.

19. When you are concerned about the things of God and how He feels about any and every situation. You want to spend time with Him.

20. Share your view on fasting in reference to scripture.

21. Write your view on Boot-Camp. See pg. 71

Chapter 4

Week 4: Staying Connecting; Relationship, Fellowship, Worship

Day – 22: You build a relationship with God mainly through prayer and studying.

Day – 23: You fellowship with other like-minded believers.

Day – 24: You must have an attitude, knowing that the Word works and there is power in the Word.

Day – 25: You become a vessel of God when you you've prepared yourself with power and authority.

Day – 26: The one fact you can state about the devil is he sets up roadblocks and you know them.

Day – 27: One thing you must establish is a prayer life.

Day – 28: When you continue your relationship with God <u>you</u> <u>will</u> <u>discover</u> <u>His</u> <u>plan</u> for you.

Relationship

1. Communication and personal a connection

2. Record your first encounter with Jesus Christ.

3. It is necessary to develop a relationship because that is how you get to know Christ and you get to learn about Him and yourself.

4. Write what did Jesus says, in John 14:6

5. Getting to know <u>Jesus</u> <u>the</u> <u>Son</u> <u>of</u> <u>God</u> is the <u>main</u> <u>source</u> of <u>stability</u> you or anyone can <u>establish</u> in your <u>relationship</u>.

6. The <u>Loving</u> relationship you <u>develop</u> will be the <u>lifeline</u> to your <u>victory</u>.

Fellowship

1. Being with other believers, it helps build character… Proverbs 27:17

2. When you commit to God, it makes it easy for the Will of God to take place in your life, to teach you also you will be obedient to Him.

3. In your own words explain 2 Corinthians 5:17.

4. You can strengthen yourself by Reading and studying the Word, being with like-minded believers, simply encouraging yourself in Lord, like David. 1 Samuel 30:6

5. "And if one prevails against him, two shall withstand him; and a threefold cord is not easily broken." Ecc. 4:12

Worship

1. True worship is a life that that honors God

2. Ways God can be worshipped see pg. 82 – 83

3. You should stay connected because you are His vessel, and the connection will bring God glory.

4. Tell in your own words what Jeremiah is talking about in Chapter 18.

5. Studying and obeying the Word of God can help you to live a victorious life.

A Sense of Purpose

1. A sense of purpose is knowing that you are fulfilling the Will of God for your life through obedience.

2. The devil always wants to detain or divert you because it will keep you from focusing on God's plan for your life. Also, the treasures you will find in His Word.

3. You give some ways you think the devil can prevent you from maturing in God.

Chapter 5

Week 5: The Test

Day – 29: What are you going to check: <u>Progress,</u> <u>accomplishments,</u> <u>challenges</u> and spiritual <u>weapons.</u>

Day – 30: You can encourage yourself by recommitting to God and the Word.

Rejoice: You have <u>learned</u> not to <u>Backslide</u> in <u>30 days</u> or <u>less!</u>

1. What matters most to the devil is, your seriousness of Christ in your heart.

2. The devil attacks you when your life, exemplifies a Christ-like lifestyle.

3. James 2:19, He goes too.

4. The devil puts stumbling blocks in our path.

5. Stumbling blocks are irritants. Those situations that upsets, aggravates or overwhelms you.

6. He uses stumbling blocks in hopes to discourage or to cause you backslide.

7. A lot of things are said from the <u>lips</u>, but it's in the <u>heart</u> where God looks and sees.

8. 1 Samuel 16:7b,

9. See Matt. 15:8

10. Write out what you think of Isaiah 29:13. People say things without really meaning it.

11. See Jer. 17:9

12. The Word and Holy Spirit help us to understand ourselves and how to believe God for victory.

13. The hope of the Believer can be found in 1 Thes. 4:17

14. In 1 Peter 4:12 – 13 warns us to not be surprised when trials and test come to think it to be strange.

15. Oppositions are creatively designed by God to help, develop and mature you. But the devil tries to use them against you, to impede growth.

16. Confusion, lies, and intimacy with God.

17.1 John 2:1

18. Prepare yourself and be able to witness about what you believe.

19. Red Flags are warning signs, to help you from Backsliding.

20. PPT – PEOPLE, PLACES AND THINGS!

21. See 2 Corinthians 6:17, 18

www.ingramcontent.com/pod-product-compliance
Lightning Source LLC
Chambersburg PA
CBHW08085612O626
46553CB00009B/2649